The ups & downs of being a grandparent

The ups & downs of being a grandparent

Tony Husband

ARCTURUS

For Pheobe and Daisy
Without you both this book wouldn't have been possible.
Love you xx

ARCTURUS

This edition published in 2017 by Arcturus Publishing Limited
26/27 Bickels Yard, 151–153 Bermondsey Street,
London SE1 3HA

Copyright © Arcturus Holdings Limited/Tony Husband

ISBN: 978-1-78404-908-9
AD004701UK

Printed in China

INTRODUCTION

Grandchildren have a remarkable power to stop you in your tracks. 'Hi, Pheebs,' I say as I meet Pheobe at the school gates to take her home when her mum and dad ring to tell me they're stuck in a traffic jam. She doesn't return my greeting. Instead she says, 'Grandad, what's with the Christmas jumper?' 'Why, don't I look cool?' I reply. 'No, people will think you're an idiot.' That's me told, I think as we head for the car.

There are many ups to being a grandparent, a hell of a lot more ups than downs to be honest. I've heard people say it's the best of both worlds because you can give them back at the end of the day. Actually I'm not that keen on handing them back, not my two anyway, Daisy and Pheobe. They are two little characters, baby Daisy and her big sister soon to be nine. Of course, it's a challenge too and of course it's a worry: they're very precious and somehow you feel an extra responsibility. So you do worry... well, I do. If worrying was an Olympic event, I would have more gold medals than Sir Steve Redgrave.

It's the magic, though, that rubs off, the magic of smiles, learning, fun, adventures, holidays, Christmas... you could go on and on, and of course there are the tumbles, the aches and pains and the tears that go with them. It's reliving childhoods, yours, your children's and now your children's children's. It's about the line of family: watching it grow, watching it thrive. If grandparenting isn't the best thing, it's got to be damn well close to it.

'How was school today?' I ask Pheobe, all strapped in in the back of the car. 'Awful, Grandad,' she says. 'You wouldn't believe what's happened!' 'What?' I ask with concern. 'Lucy Hegginbottom didn't speak to me, not once!!' 'Oh dear,' I say as worry lines furrow my brow. Why? I wonder.

Tony Husband

PS: 'Pheobe' is the correct spelling here.

5

'... and here's a list of things she doesn't like to eat.'

'Yes, they're fine. Your dad's in the garden
keeping an eye on them.'

'I wish I had that sort of control over him.'

'It's a text from Dad: "Baby has just coughed.
Should I take him to A&E?"'

'Bit over the top with the airplane feeding-the-baby technique, aren't we?'

'Grandma, Grandad just said a rude word.'

'For heaven's sake, Dad, lots of mums breastfeed in public.'

'Football, Grandad?! Don't you know One Direction
are on the other channel?'

16

'Grandma, why are you a lot older than my other grandma?'

'Okay? We went to the park, fed the ducks
and went straight home, right?'

'Have you been nibbling at his rusks again?'

'Okay, children, where have you buried Grandad?'

'Oh, hi... listen, you'll really laugh when you see your Tom.'

'Try not to wake your grandad, James, he's having a nap.'

'Yes, we're ready for her. Your dad's just doing a safety check on the playpen.'

'Hi, Mum... she wants her friends to stop over too. That okay?'

'C'mon, Grandad, round the garden again.'

'Grandma, can you get Grandad off my Xbox?'

'Grandad, I want a wee.'

'We love having our grandchildren round.'

'Grandad, Grandma, you'll be disgusted when you hear how little my mum and dad give me for pocket money.'

'Grandma, I think Grandad may have fallen in the piranha tank.'

'999... how do you change a nappy?'

'Yes, they're fine, just bathing them.'

'Had my grandaughter round today and I can now proudly recite the name of every member of One Direction.'

'Aw... has Grandma found you ickle peggie?'

'... I said, who wants to help Grandad clean his car?'

'See, Grandad likes it!'

'Mum, Dad, Grandad says I can take his old drum kit
home with us!!'

'Grandad, can I please go to sleep now?'

'Grandma, Mummy gave me this letter to give to you.'

'Our grandchild? No, we thought he was your grandchild.'

'Grandad, I don't know which is worse, your jokes or your singing.'

'Becci, stop pestering Grandma. She's very old.'

'Apparently, we're going by bus because Grandma and Grandad
have free bus passes.'

'Just one more, Grandad!'

'Grandad wants to give you a piano lesson, Tom.
Now, where have you hidden the piano?'

'If Mum and Dad split up, I'm staying with Dad 'cos he's well better than Mum at computer games.'

'Hi, Dad. Could you have them for the afternoon?
You weren't doing anything, were you?'

'Hi, Mummy... Grandad and Grandma have bought me a hamster
to bring home... Yes, of course you can speak to them.'

'Hope you don't mind, but he needs to practise his tuba
for the school band.'

'We went on the bobs, dodgems, roundabout, waltzers,
then we had to come home because Grandad was sick.'

'I was saying to Phillip the other night, your mum and dad
get to see a lot of him, don't they?'

'Look, your grandad's finishing his soup.'

'(sigh)... I wish you had a stairlift, Grandma.'

'Hi, love... Yes, they're fine. They're playing with your dad.'

'Hi, we're not back too late, are we?'

'My daughter asked if I could introduce him to golf.'

'We're going for a walk? But, Grandma, Grandad... er... erm...
a walk??'

'Right, Grandad. Matt Higgins' grandad played for United.
Have you ever done anything I can boast about?'

'And I remember changing your mummy's nappy
and seeing her little, pink botty.'

'I think Mummy and Daddy are trying for a baby.
That's why they want me out of the way, Grandma.'

'Hi, Grandad,
we're here!!'

'Double cheeseburger with fries and sauce, a banana milk shake and jam donut, and whatever you want to go...'

'Grandad got in a fight with another grandad.
I've never been so embarrassed.'

'Our Debbie says she wants to be a ballerina.'

'Grandad, you're a man of the world...'

'Well, what's that word Grandad uses when we get stuck
behind a caravan?'

'Stop!!! We've left him in the trolley.'

'I'm not sure where this government are going with their fiscal policies.'

'Tag, Grandad, you're it.'

'Daddy's new 4x4 has got television screens in the back
so we can watch films.'

'I'm building Grandad a Minecraft pub, Grandma.'

'Aw look, she's at the age to sit up and fall over.'

'You're always Manchester United.'

'Ben Hur again, Grandad, Ben Hur... just like yesterday!!!'

'I think he's still hungry, sweetheart.'

'Grandad's stuck in the slide.'

'... his middle name will be Maurice after my dad.'

'Erm... I wasn't ready. Bowl again.'

'Goodnight??!!! Grandad tells me a story.'

'Could you please pass my drink... please!?'

'Oh, *wow!* Grandad said they're going to buy me either a horse
or a goldfish for my birthday.'

'Wow! Golf's easy, isn't it, Grandad?'

'Grandma, Mum said I have to help you round the house,
but you look totally in control to me.'

"'Scuse me, you dropped this."

'My grandad's as old as the hills.'

'Look, Grandad, there's your other house.'

'I did this of you both.'

'My Billy's very much like my dad. Isn't he, Mum?'

'Grandma, Grandad, it's breakfast time.'

'Tonight I'll tell you the story of the Treble-winning team.'

'Oh, stop showing off, Richard.'

'Grandad was telling me about when he walked on the Moon.'

'Grandad dressed me this morning. Why do you ask?'

'Grandad, it's not so much me being brilliant at computer games as you being pathetic.'

'Well, Grandad and Grandma said I can have one.'

'Can one of you run me over to Grandad's?
He's struggling with his DVD player again.'

'Hi, Mum, we're back. Gran's pancakes are well better than yours!'

'Grandad and Grandma must be well old:
they still read books.'

With you in a sec.. just putting fertiliser on the rhubarb.
We put custard on ours.

'Don't go too fast now. Your grandad used to be a policeman.'

'And if you ask Grandma nicely, she might tell you about the Birds and Bees.'

'Forget the Bees, Grandad, tell me about the Birds.'

'Hi, Mum. You should have seen Grandad changing Daisy's nappy.
It was hilarious.'

'Hi, Love. Does Oscar want to come round?
His grandad's bought him a Scalextric.'

'He's got his grandad's eyes.'

'He's fine. I've just left him in the garden
playing with the hose.'

'If you get cold during the night, Pet, just shout and
I'll put another cat on your bed.'

'How was school?'
'Awful, got woman problems again.'

'He's got a bit of a stomach upset, so we've brought
a few extra nappies.'

"Scuse me!... 'SCUSE ME!!!...
Your snoring's keeping me awake!'

'Not being funny, Grandma, but I can walk faster than this...'

'C'mon, Grandad. C'mon, Grandad.'

'Wow, Grandma, how huge is your underwear!'

'He's been great. Only been sick twice
and weed on me once.'

'This is the playroom your dad's created for him, Darling.'

'Grandma, your cake was truly delicious.
Wouldn't it be totally awesome if there was some left!'

'Grandad's in trouble with Grandma. He spent a pony on the gee gees, or was it the other way round?'

'Grandad says I'm a lot smarter than you were at my age.'

'Oh, hi... I couldn't find his potty,
so I used one of your bowlers.'

'It's hypocritical of you to tell me off for being naughty when
I've heard what you were like at my age from my grandparents.'

'You're right. He's making a Minecraft snowman.'

'My grandad races pigeons apparently. I can't see him winning
'cos he's got a gammy leg.'

'Hi, Mum. Yes, Grandma's here, but Grandad's gone off
to the pub yet again.'

'Grandad, if you ever need to talk, I'm here for you.'